Rainforest

Tricia Oktober

Hodder
Children's
Books
Australia

The towering green canopy of the northern rainforest rises above the lush tangled spaces below, shielding the lower levels of the forest from the fierce heat of the tropical sun. In the moist green gloom of the forest floor, a swiftly flowing creek tumbles over moss and fern-covered rocks into a pool of clear water.

Suddenly the gentle sounds of the rainforest are shattered! The screeching whine of chainsaws drowns out the music of the little creek. The sounds of destruction shake the earth: a huge tree falls, cracking and splintering branches as it topples, tearing at the undergrowth and crushing everything in its line of fall. The far-off drone of machinery echoes into the depths of the forest until the end of the day.

As daylight begins to fade, the machines fall silent. In the stillness of the evening, life resumes in the three levels of the rainforest. Large beetles forage for food, their wings making a soft whirring hum as they fly. Dusk settles over the land. Little bats dart about and leaf-shaped katydids join the frogs on the forest floor in a chorus of sounds.

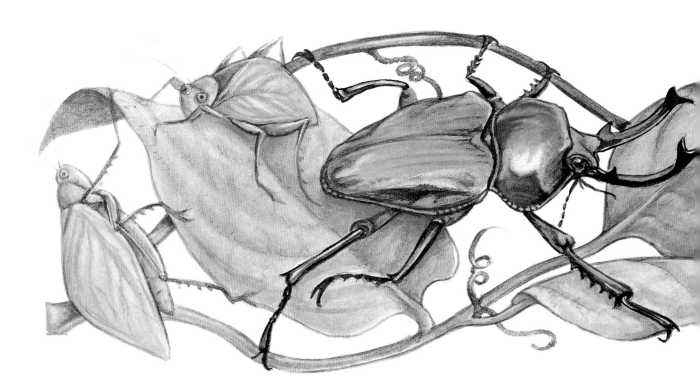

As darkness falls, the forest is filled with activity, for night is the busiest time. The blackness is lit from moment to moment by the bright blinking lights of fire-flies, which are, in fact, little beetles. Strange sounds fill the dark as creatures wake and begin to search for food.

Rustling through the leaves, snorting and scratching at tree trunks, the small striped possum hunts for wood-grubs and insects. Using the sharp claw on its elongated finger, it pokes and probes amongst the tangled roots of an orchid.

Large clumps of orchids and ferns grow along the moss- and lichen-covered branches and tree trunks. They are epiphytes, plants that grow near to the light and rely for food and moisture on what their spreading anchor roots can trap during rainfalls; they do not harm the trees. The little striped possum often uses clumps of these plants for a bed when it sleeps during the day.

High up in the tree-tops, long-tailed pygmy possums scamper about in the dark, searching for nectar. These mouse-sized marsupials use their long tails as both balancing rod and safety line as they nimbly run amongst the branch tips and sprays of blossoms.

Among the many flowering trees in the rainforest, some are perfumed only at night, to attract nectar-eating insects which pollinate the blossoms as they feed. Small green tree-frogs are attracted to insects foraging in the flowers. The little frogs clamber about, using their long legs and suction pads on their fingers and toes to grip the smooth surface of leaves and twigs. Both the frogs and pygmy possums are preyed upon by night-hunting tree snakes and owls.

A sudden tropical downpour sends the small possums to shelter beneath large drooping leaves. The rain is heavy but does not last long, and they soon resume their feeding.

A new day dawns. Early morning mists leave the forest wet and dripping. The tangled stems of vines, some as thick as a finger, others as big around as a person, climb and loop from the dimly lit forest floor, up to the light of the tree-tops.

Brightly coloured kingfishers perch above the creek, their keen eyes watchful for a yabby or small fish. A cassowary pushes through the tangled growth to the little creek, which is already turning dark with the mud that has run downstream from where the logging machinery has disturbed the soil.

The cassowary is flightless and lives on the forest floor, eating fruits that fall to the ground. Though not as tall as its relative, the emu, it is much heavier, and is bad-tempered and aggressive, with powerful legs and dagger-like toe nails. The sudden noise of the machines beginning another day's work startles the big bird. It thrusts its neck forward and, using the bony helmet on its head to part the undergrowth, turns and flees into the thick forest.

The logging machines drone on for the rest of the day. The forest creatures try to escape the din, going deeper into the green gloomy depths, seeking refuge. Clouds cover the sun, but even the downpour that follows fails to stop the machines from working. The soil, dislodged by uprooted trees and churned by heavy wheels, turns to sloppy mud and the erosion trickles down the forest floor. Heavy showers fall intermittently all day, driving earthworms to the surface, and forcing many creatures to look for dry hiding places.

Some animals, like Boyds forest dragon, ignore the wet. Perched on a tree-trunk like a small prehistoric monster, the forest dragon spies the earthworms and leaps to the ground. Upright on its spindly legs, it runs awkwardly towards the worms, snaffling them up with its big fleshy tongue. It returns to its favourite perch and remains motionless, waiting for insects. It is not a very active lizard and usually waits for its prey to come close enough to catch.

Ants are a favourite snack.

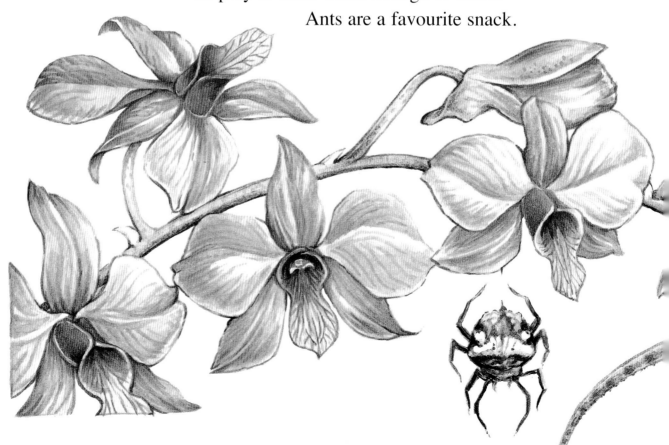

Many different species of ants live in the forest. Some cultivate fungi, creating mushroom farms in their underground nests.

Green ants make nests in trees, which they construct from leaves that are still growing. They make 'ant-chains', each ant gripping another's body in its jaws, to pull a leaf into place. Then rows of worker ants hold the leaf still, while others hurry over with little grub-like ant larvae which can make silk. The workers dab the ant-grubs against both sides of the leaf edges and bind the leaves together. The ant-grubs are not harmed and are returned to the nursery to develop into workers.

The nest of a small brown ant is a remarkable plant called the ant house plant. The entire inside of the plant is a network of chambers and galleries similar to other ant nests. The plant is an epiphyte and grows on tree trunks. Neither the ant nor the plant can exist without each other.

Each day the man-made noises come closer, vibrating through the forest. The sounds disturb large butterflies feeding on nectar in the blossoms. Most butterflies fly in the morning and feed while the air is still cool. Some flutter about the blossoms, some skip from flower to flower, while others glide gracefully over the tree tops. When the sun is at its hottest, they hide in the depths of the forest. The undersides of their wings are dark and patterned so they are well camouflaged while resting.

One of the most beautiful butterflies is the Ulysses, a large butterfly of an incredible metallic blue and black. The largest Australian butterfly is the birdwing. The male birdwing is coloured with brilliant greens, but the female, although larger, is dark with very little colour.

As the afternoon cools, the butterflies resume their feeding and the machines drone on for the rest of the day.

Although the rainforest supports huge numbers of different creatures, there are never large, permanent populations of any one species. Each species has its own small territory and some species cannot be found in any other part of the forest. The noise and destruction create enormous stress throughout the forest. To escape, creatures move away from their own territory but, in doing so, invade other territories and compete for food and shelter. The fragile balance of the forest begins to be upset.

As dusk falls, a female Hercules moth bursts out of her leafy cocoon lined with silk. The female Hercules moth is the largest insect in Australia and the largest moth in the world. She leaves the cocoon and waits for her crumpled wings to expand and dry, then flies up to the canopy. With her huge wings outstretched she waits in the dark for her mate. Although the male is slightly smaller, his hind wings have long, elegantly tapered tails. With his large feathery antennae the male picks up the perfume of the female from the air, often travelling long distances to find her.

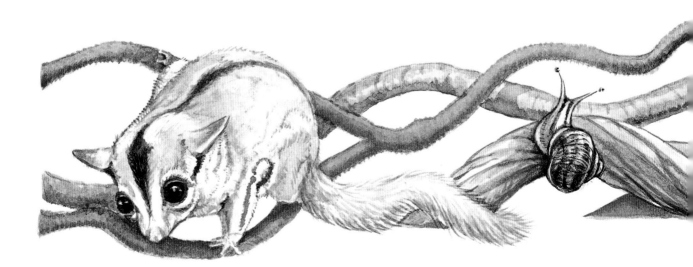

The sweet fragrance of honey-laden blossoms wafts in the warm night air and small blossom-bats are quick to locate it, their calls ringing clearly through the forest. Like all fruit- or flower-eating bats, blossom-bats do not navigate using ultrasound, but rely on sight and smell. They feed only on pollen and nectar, licking it out with their long tongues which have little brushes on the tip to collect the pollen. Since flying uses a lot of energy, the blossom-bats must eat larger quantities of food than a ground animal of similar size. As they eat, they pollinate the flowers they are feeding on and are important to the production of fruit and seeds of rainforest trees. The little blossom-bats feed until nearly dawn before they roost.

Many other creatures are also attracted to the honey smell of the blossoms. A small gecko lizard, which only eats insects and hunts in the dark, waits to ambush the moths that arrive to sip on the nectar in the flowers.

Just before dawn, the forest is filled with leathery flapping wings and much squawking as hundreds of flying-foxes and fruit-bats return to their 'camp' in the forest. Large camps are formed when food is available. When food is scarce, the camps break up into small groups. During the night the animals feed on soft fruits, which they crush in their mouths, swallowing only the juice and spitting out the rest.

A green ring-tail possum, awakened by the noisy arrival, goes in search of food. Although mostly a night animal, the ring-tail does move about and feed during the day. Its unusual green colour, created by the mixture of black, grey, yellow and white hairs in its fur, camouflages it perfectly in the shadowy green forest.

After eating some fig leaves, the small possum looks for a place to sleep. On an open branch it sits and coils up its tail, and with front paws under its chin, tucks its head tightly into its belly and sleeps upright.

Long before the hour when the machines start working, different man-made noises echo in the forest. Many loud voices shout in anger. All day the machines remain silent, but the loud voices yell on and off all day.

The noisy outbursts sounding through the trees interrupt a pair of feeding wompoo pigeons. Like many of the rainforest doves, the wompoo is brightly coloured and eats whatever fruits it can find.

Figs are a major food source for many creatures. A large number of different species of wild figs grow throughout the forest, and fruit from one or another is always ripe. Some fig trees are huge, like the giant strangler fig tree, and some are slender and more like vines.

The smallest parrot in Australia, the tiny double-eyed fig parrot, eats only wild figs. A timid little bird, it lives nowhere but in rainforests.

As the day fades, the human voices become muffled and when darkness falls, light and smoke mark the area of a camp-site.

In the days that follow, the machines remain silent. The sounds of human voices, however, make a constant murmur through the forest, blending with the music of the little creek as it tumbles over mossy rocks and spills into the pool of muddy water. The days turn into weeks.

Then suddenly one morning the wailing of sirens shatters the stillness and once again angry shouts and screams fill the air. The engines roar to life and, for a while, drown out all the other sounds. Gradually the mechanical noise fades as the machines, vehicles and people depart. An eerie silence follows. It lasts until darkness falls and the normal night-time noises of the forest resume.

In the total darkness of the forest the lesser sooty owl glides on silent wings, searching for prey. The small owl manoeuvres its flight through the thick forest, and lands vertically, clinging to a tree-trunk, a useful skill in a rainforest, which has few horizontal branches.

Early morning birdcalls herald a new day. Brightly coloured birds poke their long curved beaks into blossoms, sipping up nectar. There is an abundance of flowers in the rainforest and many of the birds are honeyeaters.

A tree kangaroo looks for a sleeping place after feeding during the night on leaves and fruit. It will spend the day asleep, crouched on a branch or in the crown of a large tree. Despite its clumsy appearance, the tree kangaroo is a good climber and uses its long tail as a balancing rod.

In the lush green canopy, most of the food for the forest is produced. There are no real seasons in a tropical rainforest, and trees of one type or another are always in fruit or coming into blossom. Fruit, flowers and leaves fall to the forest floor, providing food for ground-dwelling birds and animals. Countless little insects, bacteria and fungi feed on the decaying litter of the forest floor. As plants die and fruits decay, the minerals they contain are returned to the soil. Nothing goes to waste in the living rainforest.

Many months pass. Nothing disturbs the forest. The water in the little creek runs clean and clear again.

A small red-legged pademelon hops along a well-worn pathway to feed on fallen fruits and fig leaves on the ground. It browses on ferns and orchids, then quickly retreats to the undergrowth as a little brown frog croaks nearby.

In the moist forest, creatures normally only found in water, glide over wet leaves. Leeches wait, ready to attach themselves to the first animal that passes. Large snails and giant millipedes feed on leaves. Enormous centipedes feed on insects.

The whole forest teems with life, but none of the creatures will ever know how close the machines came to destroying their home. They will never know of the brave people who risked so much, or of those who fought so hard for this forest to be … PROTECTED WILDERNESS.

NOTES FOR PARENTS AND TEACHERS

A rainforest is best described as a dense evergreen forest occurring in areas of high humidity and heavy rainfall. The vegetation of a rainforest grows in three layers: the canopy (tallest trees), the understorey (vines and smaller trees), and the forest floor.

The word 'rainforest' conjures up a mental picture of tropical jungles, but in Australia rainforests can be broadly grouped into tropical, sub-tropical, warm temperate and cool temperate forests. Within this range, there are more than twenty identifiable types of rainforest that do not fit the image of lush jungle.

Before white settlement, Australia had seventy-five percent more rainforest than it does today. The total rainforest remaining, including wet, dry, hot and cold types, is about two million hectares. Wet, tropical rainforests are limited to areas of northern Queensland, and much of this has been cleared, leaving isolated fragments in many places. Although large, valuable areas remain, agriculture, timber and other development continue to threaten them. Selective logging is supposed to allow for regeneration; unfortunately, the expectations cannot yet be tested, because a sufficient interval after logging has simply not passed.

Regeneration to the same level of diversity and plant complexity, may take more than one hundred years. Breaks in the closed canopy remove sun and wind protection and encourage die-back. Trees unable to cope with the prolonged exposure die, and soil, no longer held by roots, washes away in heavy tropical rains. Severe erosion and a decrease in overall fertility results. Exotic weeds and feral animals make inroads into the newly opened clearings, disturbing the forest floor and destroying the understorey, which also prevents any chance of regeneration. Rainforests cannot be adequately protected without conserving the surrounding hardwood eucalyptus forests that act as a buffer against fire; an event which rarely ever penetrates a rainforest.

Many edible fruits, Macadamia nuts, rubber and quinine all come from rainforest plants, which have an untapped potential for new pharmacological and commercial products. The rainforest is a living laboratory and hides a storehouse of information for the future. As such, the implications for the human race are enormous and we must ensure the survival of these unique environments.

A Hodder Children's Book

First published in Australia and New Zealand in 1998
by Hodder Headline Australia Pty Limited,
(A member of the Hodder Headline Group)
10-16 South Street, Rydalmere NSW 2116

Published in paperback 1998

Tricia Oktober's artwork is available from Ozart Gallery, Katoomba, and Seasons Gallery, North Sydney.

National Library of Australia Cataloguing-in-Publication data

Oktober, Tricia.
Rainforest

ISBN 0 7336 0937 6.
1. Rainforests - Australia - Juvenile literature. 2. Rainforest
plants - Australia - Juvenile literature. 3. Rainforest animals -
Australia - Juvenile literature. I. Title.
577.340994

Printed in Hong Kong